Arctic Ocean

30°E 60° 90° 120° 150°

A S I A

EUROPE

AFRICA

ARABIA

Pacific

Ocean

Indian

Ocean

AUSTRALIA

NEW ZEALAND

ANTARCTICA

New Zealand

Barbara Jackson

Vaughan Wood and Simon Milne, Consultants

NATIONAL GEOGRAPHIC

WASHINGTON, D.C.

Contents

Foreword

Now Zealand's islands are some of the youngest in the world. They were formed by a violent uplifting of the Earth's crust. When humans first inhabited the dramatic new landscape, less than a thousand years ago, they found unique flora and fauna, including flightless parrots, the nocturnal kiwi, and the world's largest insect.

New Zealanders, or "Kiwis," have been shaped by their remoteness from the rest of the world. The first migrants, the Maori, developed a sophisticated society and culture. Discovery and occasional contact by Europeans in the 1600s and 1700s led to a flood of migrants from Great Britain in the 1800s, and to the rapid integration of New Zealand into the global economy. The country's growth was built around the export of raw materials and agricultural products to the British "motherland." While the young nation prospered, many Maori lost their lands and died from diseases introduced by the "Pakeha" (colonists).

Being located on the "edge" of the world has forced New Zealanders to become innovative. The country has led the world in many areas of social policy. It was the first nation to give women the vote, in 1893, and introduced a full welfare state system in the 1930s. The old dependence on Great Britain has made way for closer links to Australia, Asia, and North America. Lamb and butter from New Zealand are now joined on the world's supermarket shelves by New Zealand wines and kiwifruit. Tourism has also grown, with more than two million international visitors a year arriving to see the nation's wild landscapes and experience its unique way of life. Maori have undergone a cultural resurgence in recent decades and are an important economic and political force within the country.

New Zealand has witnessed a lot in its short history—and there is no doubt that many challenges and opportunities lie ahead that will require Kiwis to maintain their tradition of innovation on the "edge." New Zealanders look forward to the challenge. In the words of a Maori proverb:

"He manga wai koia kia kore e whitikia."
("It is a big river indeed that cannot be crossed.")

▲ **The Sky Tower that dominates Auckland's skyline was built at the end of the 20th century to broadcast TV and radio signals.**

Simon Milne
Faculty of Applied Humanitie Auckland
University of Technology

Land
of the
Long White
Cloud

NEW ZEALAND IS A VERY REMOTE PLACE. It is more than 1,000 miles (1,600 km) southeast of its nearest neighbor, Australia. The same distance in all other directions, there is nothing apart from a few tiny islands and the South Pacific Ocean. No human set foot on New Zealand until about 1,000 years ago. They were the Maori, who canoed across the ocean, navigating by the stars—nobody is quite sure where they came from. The Maori name for the country is *Aotearoa*, meaning "The Land of the Long White Cloud." Today's New Zealanders originally come from Europe, Africa, and Asia, and they are rightly proud of the land's varied, volcanic scenery. They have a fun name for their nation: Godzone—short for "God's Own Country."

◀ **People take a swim in the ocean at Cathedral Cove on New Zealand's North Island. The cove is named for the large cave that connects it to the neighboring bay.**

WHAT'S THE WEATHER LIKE?

New Zealand is made up of two main islands, known as the North Island and the South Island. They are divided by the Cook Strait. Although the islands run 1,000 miles (1,600 km) from top to bottom, the whole country has a mild climate. The ocean surrounding the country ensures that extreme weather is kept to a minimum.

The warmest part of the country is the north, which is also the wettest. The whole of New Zealand is quite wet, though, and rain falls at all times of year. The coldest places are the mountains that dominate the South Island. They are covered in snow for most of the winter.

The country lies in the Roaring Forties, an area of the world where winds blow from west to east and can switch from being a gentle breeze to a strong gale with little warning. Labels on this map and similar maps throughout this book identify most of the places pictured in each chapter.

Fast Facts

OFFICIAL NAME: New Zealand /Aotearoa (Maori)
FORM OF GOVERNMENT: Parliamentary democracy
CAPITAL: Wellington
POPULATION: 4,236,000
OFFICIAL LANGUAGES: English/Maori
MONETARY UNIT: New Zealand dollar
AREA: 103,883 square miles (269,057 square km)
HIGHEST POINT: Mount Cook 12,316 feet (3,754 meters)
LOWEST POINT: Pacific Ocean, sea level, 0 feet (0 m)
MAJOR MOUNTAIN RANGES: Southern Alps, Kaikoura Ranges
MAJOR RIVERS: Waikato, Clutha, Rangitaiki, Wanganui Manawatu, Buller, Rakaia, Waitaki, Waiau

Average Temperature & Rainfall

Average High/Low Temperatures; Yearly Rainfall
AUCKLAND: 75° F (24° C) / 48° F (9° C); 45 in (115 cm)
ROTORUA: 75° F (24° C) / 59° F (13° C); 55 in (141 cm)
WELLINGTON: 68° F (20° C) / 43° F (6° C); 48 in (122 cm)
CHRISTCHURCH: 72° F (22° C) / 37° F (3° C); 25 in (64 cm)
QUEENSTOWN: 72° F (22° C) / 34° F (1° C); 31 in (81 cm)

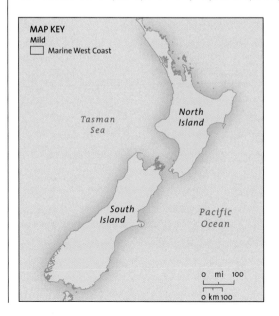

MAP KEY
Mild
☐ Marine West Coast

Tasman Sea

North Island

South Island

Pacific Ocean

0 mi 100

0 km 100

Three Kings
Islands

Cape Reinga   North Cape

Northland

BEACH AND CLIFFS,
page 2, 6–7

Great Barrier
Island

Hauraki Gulf

SAILBOAT MASTS
AND CITYSCAPE,
page 13

Coromandel
Peninsula

Cathedral Cove

Auckland   Hot Water
Beach

Waikato   Bay of
Plenty

BOILING MUD,
page 14
AND

Hamilton   Tauranga

Mt. Tarawera
1111m

East
Cape

WOMAN COOKS FOOD IN HOT SPRING,
page 15

Waitomo Caves   Rotorua

CAVE WITH
GLOWING ROOF,
page 14

Wairakei

Rangitaiki

Gisborne

GEOTHERMAL
POWER PLANT,
page 15

Mt. Taranaki
2518m

Lake
Taupo

NORTH
ISLAND

Mahia
Peninsula

Mount
Ruapehu
2797m

Rangitikei

Hawke
Bay

Napier

Hastings

Tasman
Sea

N E W

Z E A L A N D

Rangitikei

Palmerston North

Cape Farewell

PERSON CLIMBS
BETWEEN ROCKS,
page 12

Tasman
Bay

Maud I.

Cook Strait

Lower Hutt
Wellington

Nelson

Cape Foulwind

Buller

Kaikoura
Clarence
Ranges

FORESTED ISLAND,
page 12

Pacific
Ocean

PEAK RISING
ABOVE CLOUDS,
page 11

Lake
Brunner

Kaikoura

Mount Cook
(Highest point in New Zealand)
12,316 ft
3,754 m

SOUTH

Southern Alps

Canterbury
Plains

Rakaia

Christchurch

Banks
Peninsula

ISLAND

Ashburton

Canterbury
Bight

Timaru

Otago Gold
Mine

Lake
Wakatipu

Waitaki

Queenstown

Oamaru

Lake
Te Anau

Fiordland

Waiau

Clutha

Dunedin

Invercargill

Foveaux Strait

SAND
DUNES,
page 10

Stewart
Island

MAP KEY

⊛   National capital

●   Selected city

+   Elevation

0   miles   100

0   km   100

Pacific
Ocean

Australasia

NEW
ZEALAND

Physical Map

RISING FROM THE SEA

Maori legend says New Zealand was fished up out of the sea by the demi-god Maui, who hauled in the North Island with his magic hook. The South Island was the canoe in which Maui sat while landing his catch, and small Stewart Island to the south was the anchor stone, keeping his boat steady. This story has a surprising resemblance to the scientific explanation of how New Zealand formed by being driven up out of the ocean by enormous volcanic forces.

▲ Grassy sand dunes cover the western shore of Stewart Island. This island is the third largest in New Zealand, and it has only 400 permanent residents.

A New Land

When the dinosaurs ruled the world 100 million years ago, New Zealand did not exist. As land goes, this country is a very young place. Although there has been land in this part of the world on and off for 500 million years, the New Zealand islands of today first appeared just 23 million years ago. The land was pushed up out of the ocean by volcanic forces—New Zealand has about 50 volcanoes, some of which still erupt from time to time. New Zealand did not emerge fully formed—it has been shifting ever since and only took its present shape 10,000 years ago.

Because New Zealand's landscape is so young, it has yet to be eroded away and smoothed down by millions of years of rain and wind. As a result the country has a huge number of spectacular landscapes crammed into an area a little smaller than the U.S. state of Colorado. In addition to the active volcanoes, there are ancient rain forests, glaciers, and

WITH AND WITHOUT WATER

Tokelau is a group of 127 islands, with three main low-lying coral atolls, in the South Pacific, almost halfway between New Zealand and Hawaii. Although Tokelau has its own government, it is a territory of New Zealand. Without money from the mainland, life on Tokelau would be very difficult. The territory is connected to the rest of the world by a ferry that travels from Samoa every two weeks. Even with funding the 1,500 islanders have several unusual problems. There is no supply of drinking water anywhere on the islands, and people carefully collect rain water in tanks and hollowed-out palm trunks. They also make a weak beer-like drink from coconut sap.

▲ Tokelau schoolboys in traditional clothes

But sometimes, the islands' problem is having too much water. With no land more than 7 feet (2 m) above sea level, Tokelau is vulnerable to high waves blown in by storms. The 2005 hurricane Cyclone Percy submerged several villages.

pools of boiling mud. About a third of the land is covered in ranges of sharp mountain peaks.

Cloud Piercer

Both the North and South Islands are divided in half by mountains. The largest range is the Southern Alps, a 300-mile (480-km) chain of mountains that runs down most of the South Island. New Zealand's highest peak,

▼ Mount Cook, the tallest peak in New Zealand, rises above the clouds covering the rest of the Southern Alps.

Mount Cook, is in the central part of the range near the west coast. In Maori this is known as Aoraki, which means "Cloud Piercer." The Alps are filled with glaciers; many feed lakes high in the mountains. In the past, the glaciers ground out deep valleys. Much of the ice has now melted, and the valleys and mountains combine to form a very rugged region. Where the mountains meet the ocean, the sea floods the glacial valleys to make inlets, or fiords. The area is named Fiordland.

▲ Maud Island, located in Marlborough Sounds, at the northern tip of the South Island

Many of the rivers running from the Southern Alps have been dammed for making electricity. Silt from the largest rivers has built up on the eastern side of the mountains, forming the fertile Canterbury Plains.

▼ A tourist climbs on Split Apple Rock near Tasman Bay, South Island.

Island of Volcanoes

The mountains of the North Island are less massive than the Southern Alps, although they formed at the same time.

The northern range runs from Wellington, the New Zealand capital, to the East Cape.

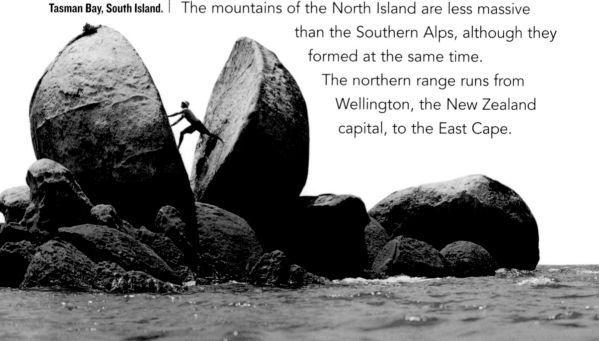

As its name suggests, Northland is in the far north of New Zealand, forming a long peninsula that points out into the Pacific. This region is warm and humid and has lush forest and mangrove swamps. At the foot of the Northland region is Auckland, the country's largest city. It is built on several volcanoes. Some are still considered active, although the last eruption 600 years ago was on an island outside the city.

At the center of the North Island is Lake Taupo, the largest body of fresh water in the country. It formed after the crater of a now-extinct volcano collapsed in on itself. Other volcanoes in the North Island are still very active. Mount Taranaki on the west coast last erupted in the 1600s. One of the world's most active

▲ Auckland is very much an oceanside city. It is built on a strip of land between two huge natural harbors, and is a world center of sailing.

volcanoes—Mount Ruapehu in the center of the country—began erupting again in late 2007.

Getting the Shakes

New Zealand lies on the boundary of two of Earth's tectonic plates—sections of crust

▲ New Zealand is famous for hot volcanic springs and pools of boiling mud.

that carry the land and seabed. As the plates rub together they sometimes make the ground shake, causing an earthquake. Earthquakes are common in New Zealand: At the end of 2007 the town of Gisborne was shaken by a large quake.

AGLOW WITH WORMS

Miles of caves lie beneath rugged hills at Waitomo, 46 miles (74 km) south of Hamilton in the North Island. Its name comes from the Maori *wai* (water) and *tomo* (hole). The highlight of the cave system is the Glowworm Cave, which is reached by boat through a huge cavern. The roof of the cave twinkles with the blue-green lights of thousands of tiny glowworms. These are not worms at all but the maggots of the fungus gnat. The insects are particularly common in the cave because of the warm and damp conditions. The maggots produce light to attract flying insect prey, which they trap in sticky silk.

▲ A boat approaches Glowworm Cave at Waitomo.

HOT HOT HOT!

New Zealand's North Island volcanic region has been a source of energy from the days when the Maori first lowered a small basket containing meat and sweet potatoes, or *kumara*, into boiling pools. Today at Hot Water Beach in the Coromandel near Auckland, vacationers gather shellfish to cook in boiling water gushing from hot sand. In the volcanic region around Rotorua, warm spring water has traditionally been used at health spas and to fill swimming pools.

The heat from the groundwater is also used to make electricity. In the 1960s the world's second-largest geothermal power plant was built at Wairakei. It used the super-hot steam from deep underground to drive generators. The steam traveled to the surface in pipes. However, by the 1980s the pressure in the system began dropping as the ground cooled down, and now the plant produces only a fraction of the electricity for which it was built.

▲ A Maori woman boils some food in the volcanic spring at Rotorua.

Both of these most recent events have caused little damage, but the same was not true in the past. In the 1880s, Lake Rotomahana was a popular tourist spot as people came to see the beautiful crystals formed by hot springs. But all that changed in 1886 when nearby Mount Tarawera erupted, blasting fireballs across the surrounding countryside. In just five hours the three villages on the lake were destroyed completely.

▼ Plumes of steam rise up from the Wairakei geothermal power plant, where steam heated by lava deep underground is used to make electricity.

A Natural Ark

NEW ZEALAND HAS WILDLIFE LIKE nowhere else on Earth. The country has been cut off from the rest of the world for so long that its plants and animals have evolved in a very different way from those in other regions.

New Zealand's islands have never been connected to a continent, and so animals could only reach them by swimming, flying, or floating there on logs. As a result there are just two types of land mammal—both of which are bats. There are no snakes at all, only two kinds of lizards, and a handful of frogs. Nearly all of the country's land animals are birds. Over the years, these winged creatures have evolved to fill in the gaps left by the missing mammals: some eat grass, others dig for worms, and many have lost the power of flight.

◀ The kakapo is the world's largest parrot. About the size of a large house cat, the kakapo cannot fly. They do climb well and scratch around for seeds and fruits.

At a Glance

NEW ARRIVALS

The arrival of people in New Zealand over the last 1,000 years or so has had a very damaging effect on New Zealand's wildlife. The Maori brought pet dogs with them in their canoes and rats also hitched a ride with them. New Zealand's unusual animals had no defense against the Maori dog, which is now itself extinct. The Maori hunted flightless birds for food, including the giant moas, which also eventually became extinct. The rats attacked New Zealand's insects, including giant crickets called wetas.

The Europeans introduced many farm animals and other damaging species, such as cats, stoats, and rabbits, which took over from the birdlife. One of the worst offenders was the possum, a marsupial from Australia, which is still a pest today.

▶ The takahe is one of the rarest birds in the world. It is a giant relative of the coot and eats tough grasses on high mountain slopes.

Species at Risk

In addition to the problems caused by introduced animals, the activities of people, such as clearing forests and draining swamps, also resulted in the loss of many species. The people of New Zealand recognized the threat to their wildlife earlier than many countries, and today New Zealand is a world leader in conservation. Many species have been saved from extinction, although their numbers are often still very low. The rarest species are protected in isolated areas of the country, such as outlying islands, which are free of rats and other damaging predators.

Species at risk include:
> Alpine weta (cricket)
> Black stilt (bird)
> Hector's dolphin
> Hooker's sea lion
> Kakapo (bird)
> Kiwi (bird)
> Southern short-tailed bat
> Stephens Island gecko (reptile)
> Takahe (bird)
> Tuatara (reptile)

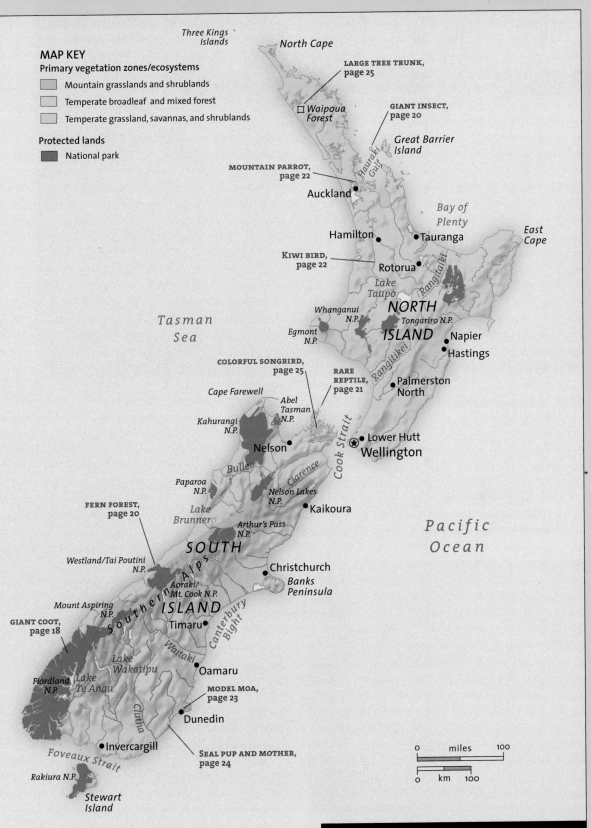

MAP KEY

Primary vegetation zones/ecosystems

Mountain grasslands and shrublands

Temperate broadleaf and mixed forest

Temperate grassland, savannas, and shrublands

Protected lands

National park

Three Kings Islands

North Cape

LARGE TREE TRUNK, page 25

☐ *Waipoua Forest*

GIANT INSECT, page 20

Great Barrier Island

MOUNTAIN PARROT, page 22

Hauraki Gulf

Auckland

Bay of Plenty

Hamilton ● ● Tauranga

East Cape

KIWI BIRD, page 22

Rotorua ● ● *Rangitaiki*

Lake Taupo

NORTH ISLAND

Whanganui N.P.

Egmont N.P.

Tongariro N.P.

● Napier

● Hastings

Tasman Sea

COLORFUL SONGBIRD, page 25

Rangitikei

RARE REPTILE, page 21

● Palmerston North

Cape Farewell

Abel Tasman N.P.

Kahurangi N.P.

Nelson

Cook Strait

★ Lower Hutt
Wellington

Buller

Clarence

Paparoa N.P.

Nelson Lakes N.P.

● Kaikoura

FERN FOREST, page 20

Lake Brunner

Arthur's Pass N.P.

Pacific Ocean

SOUTH ISLAND

Southern Alps

Westland/Tai Poutini N.P.

Aoraki/ Mt. Cook N.P.

● Christchurch

Banks Peninsula

Mount Aspiring N.P.

GIANT COOT, page 18

Timaru ●

Canterbury Bight

Waitaki

Mount Aspiring N.P.

Lake Wakatipu

● Oamaru

Fiordland N.P.

Lake Te Anau

Clutha

MODEL MOA, page 23

● Dunedin

● Invercargill

Foveaux Strait

SEAL PUP AND MOTHER, page 24

Rakiura N.P.

Stewart Island

0 miles 100

0 km 100

Vegetation & Ecosystems Map

▲ The forests of New Zealand are filled with ferns the size of trees.

▼ At 2.5 ounces (70 g), the giant weta is the world's heaviest insect.

A New Beginning

When New Zealand rose from the sea, it had no plants or animals. Very soon, however, New Zealand came to life, as seeds and spores blown on the wind settled to the ground and sprouted into the first plants. Animals such as insects and birds arrived by air as well, mostly blown in by strong gales. A few species, such as frogs and lizards, probably drifted there from nearby islands on rafts of vegetation.

Feet on the Ground

The new arrivals had an easy life at first. Unlike in the areas where the birds had come from, here there

ALMOST A DINOSAUR

One of the country's oldest inhabitants is the tuatara. This animal looks like a large lizard, but it is actually a separate type of reptile. Tuataras evolved at the same time as the dinosaurs but have died out elsewhere. They once lived across New Zealand, but today they are found only on a few islands off the coast. Only there are the reptiles safe from introduced pests like rats and weasels.

Tuataras grow to about 2 feet (60 cm) long and live for more than 100 years. They live on insects and birds' eggs. There are about 60,000 tuataras left, mainly on Stephens Island in Malborough Sounds. Conservationists are trying to breed more tuataras, but it is a difficult task. The females do not breed until they are 25 and then only produce one egg every two years.

▲ The name *tuatara* means "peaks along the back" in Maori. It refers to the spikes on the spine and tail.

were no threats from large hunting animals. The birds had wings and were suited to life in the air, but there was also food to be had on the ground. Normally this would have been the home of mammals such as mice or raccoons, but in New Zealand birds evolved to live in their place.

Many of the birds lost the power of flight—they no longer needed to flap into the air to escape predators. Even New Zealand's bats—the only mammals to make the ocean crossing—sometimes hunt on the ground. They can still fly but have strong legs and claws on their wings with which to push and pull themselves along.

New Zealand insects also evolved to replace mammals. The wetas, large relatives of crickets, are the nearest thing the insect world has to a mouse.

There are 70 species, and all of them live only in New Zealand. Just like mice, they eat seeds and have big jaws for cracking hard seed cases.

The alpine weta is one of the few animals of any kind able to survive being frozen. The insect lives high in the Southern Alps and spends the winter covered in ice. Chemicals in its blood stop the insect's body from freezing solid.

▲ Keas often visit the parking lots in scenic areas, where they rip at rubber windshield seals and snatch food from people's hands.

The Unique Kiwi

New Zealanders call themselves "Kiwis" after their most famous flightless birds. A small relation of the emu and extinct moa, the kiwi sleeps for up to 20 hours a day, and spends a few hours each night eating worms, beetles, berries, and crayfish. Its wings are very small and hard to see among its spiky feathers. The kiwi is one of the few birds with a strong sense of smell. It sniffs the ground with nostrils located at the end of its long, pointed beak, which it uses to dig out food from soil and leaves.

Kiwis also have sharp hearing, and will attack other birds that come too close. Their eggs weigh a quarter of the female adult bird. The chick breaks out of the egg using its

▼ The kiwi has a long beak for pulling food out of the soil.

SO LONG, MIGHTY MOA

Half of New Zealand's animals have become extinct in the last 1,000 years. They include huge birds called moas. When the Maori arrived, there were about 20 species in New Zealand. The smallest was the size of a turkey, while the largest was more than 10 feet (3 m) tall.

The Maori hunted the birds for meat and they used the bones to make hooks and spearheads. The moas' immense 10-inch- (25-cm) long eggshells were used as water flasks. Moas were fast runners and fought with powerful kicks, but even the large species could not escape human hunters. The largest moas became extinct in the 1500s, while the smaller species finally disappeared in the late 1700s.

▲ A man sizes up a full-scale model of a giant moa at a wildlife park in Dunedin.

feet, and it is one of the few birds that is able to live on its own right away. It is thought there are fewer than 75,000 wild kiwis left. People only see them in "kiwi houses" in zoos, where the birds live in dark enclosures so they think it is night, even when it is still day outside.

▼ New Zealand's cliffs have many colonies of albatrosses, birds that spend all year at sea before coming to land to produce chicks.

Mountain Parrot

In most places parrots are known for being colorful birds that chatter in the treetops, but not in New Zealand. For example, the kea is a large, drab green bird that lives in the mountains—the only parrot found at high altitude, where it survives by eating insects and picking at

the flesh of dead animals. The kea is an inquisitive bird and a fearless one. It can afford to be since it has a powerful slicing beak, which can give a painful bite. Keas have even been known to kill sheep.

"More Pork" and Other Songs

New Zealand's only owl species, the morepork, is named for its unique call, which sounds like a person loudly ordering "more pork!" The morepork is one of the main native hunters—it preys largely on wetas.

Another noisy New Zealand bird is the beautiful tui. This bird gives a bell-like call and can be easily spotted because of the fluffy white feathers on its dark throat. Tuis can be seen in gardens as well as in "the bush," the New Zealand name for forest.

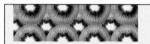

ARRIVING BY SEA

Although few land mammals reached New Zealand naturally, the islands are home to many sea mammals. Pilot and humpback whales visit every year during their journey to breed, while sperm whales are visible off Kaikoura on the South Island. Orca, or killer whales, are regulars along the coast, where they feed on the four dolphin species living in New Zealand's waters. New Zealand fur seals are the most common sea mammals. They haul out on beaches all around New Zealand's coasts.

▲ A mother fur seal barks a warning to protect her pup.

FATHER OF THE FOREST

The Waipoua Forest, in Northland province, is home to a very precious tree. The Maori name for it is *Te Matua Ngahere*, which means "The Father of the Forest." It is a kauri tree, a species found only in New Zealand, and it is thought to be the oldest tree in the country—at least 2,000 years old. It is also a huge specimen with a trunk that is more than 16 feet (5 m) across. The tallest tree in the country is another kauri nearby, named *Tane Mahuta* after the Maori forest god. It stands 167 feet (51 m) high.

The totara is another much-loved New Zealand species. The tree lives for 1,000 years, and at funerals, New Zealanders often say of the deceased that "a mighty totara has fallen."

▲ The huge trunk of a kauri tree dwarfs the person standing beneath it.

Forests and Flowers

Before Europeans settlers came to New Zealand in the 19th century two-thirds of the country was covered by evergreen forest. All that remains of this today is on steep slopes, in hard-to-reach places, or in reserves.

New Zealand's national emblem is the ponga, a silver fern that is one of the many types that grow in the forests. The national flower is from the kowhai tree. Its name means "yellow" in Maori, and that is the color of its blossoms. At Christmas, which is in summer in New Zealand, red flowers appear on pohutukawa trees, across the northern part of the country.

▼ The tui is also called the parson bird because its white throat looks like the collar worn by some clergymen.

The *Young Country*

APART FROM ANTARCTICA, New Zealand was the last major landmass to be explored by humankind. According to Maori tradition, New Zealand was discovered in A.D. 925 by Kupe, a Polynesian chief who fled his home island of Hawaiki. Kupe had left a cousin to drown and made off with the cousin's widow in a canoe. On the voyage that followed, Kupe came across New Zealand before returning home to encourage his people to move there. A few centuries later the ancestors of the various Maori tribes began to make the long and treacherous voyage from Hawaiki to New Zealand. No one is really sure where Hawaiki might have been. Some suggest it was one of the islands near Tahiti, to the northeast. Currently archaeologists believe that the Maori began settling in New Zealand around the year 1250.

◀ An artist's impression of a double canoe bringing Maori to New Zealand

ANCIENT CIVILIZATIONS

▼ Maori did not know how to make metal objects, so their fortified villages, such as this one from the 1920s, were constructed largely of wood.

Wherever their homeland of Hawaiki was, experts believe that Maori are Polynesians and are related to the people who had slowly spread throughout the islands of the Pacific Ocean, probably originally from Southeast Asia.

Once the Maori had arrived in New Zealand in their long outrigger wooden canoes, they had to adapt to the cooler climate and unfamiliar food sources in their new homeland.

In addition to hunting large wild birds, Maori also kept gardens and fished. As birds became extinct and competition for other resources increased, the Maori developed an ordered society of tribes and clans. The tribes often went to war over the control of land, and warriors were highly respected members of each community. People lived in fortified villages, known as *pa*. The earthwork remains of pa can still be seen in many parts of the country.

Time line

This chart shows some of the important dates in the history of New Zealand. Nobody knows when the first Polynesian settlers arrived. The latest estimate is about 750 years ago.

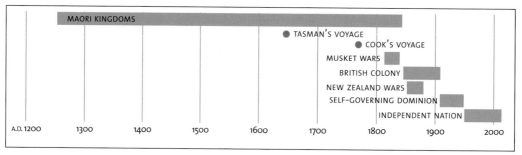

MAORI KINGDOMS
● TASMAN'S VOYAGE
● COOK'S VOYAGE
MUSKET WARS
BRITISH COLONY
NEW ZEALAND WARS
SELF-GOVERNING DOMINION
INDEPENDENT NATION

A.D. 1200 | 1300 | 1400 | 1500 | 1600 | 1700 | 1800 | 1900 | 2000

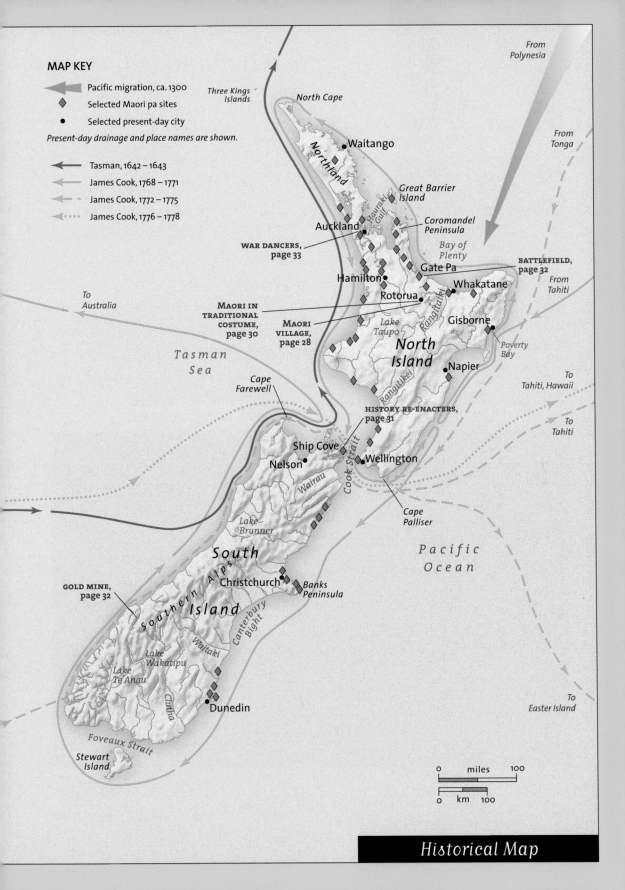

MAP KEY

◄── Pacific migration, ca. 1300

◆ Selected Maori pa sites

● Selected present-day city

Present-day drainage and place names are shown.

◄─── Tasman, 1642 – 1643

◄─── James Cook, 1768 – 1771

◄- - - James Cook, 1772 – 1775

◄····· James Cook, 1776 – 1778

From Polynesia

Three Kings Islands

North Cape

Northland

From Tonga

●Waitango

Great Barrier Island

Hauraki Gulf

To Australia

WAR DANCERS, page 33

●Auckland

Coromandel Peninsula

Bay of Plenty

BATTLEFIELD, page 32

From Tahiti

Hamilton●

Gate Pa

Whakatane

Tasman Sea

MAORI IN TRADITIONAL COSTUME, page 30

MAORI VILLAGE, page 28

Rotorua●

Rangitaiki

Gisborne●

Lake Taupo

North Island

Poverty Bay

To Tahiti, Hawaii

●Napier

Rangitikei

To Tahiti

Cape Farewell

HISTORY RE-ENACTERS, page 31

Ship Cove●

Nelson●

Wellington●

Cook Strait

Cape Palliser

Wairau

Pacific Ocean

Lake Brunner

GOLD MINE, page 32

South Alps

Christchurch●

●Banks Peninsula

Canterbury Bight

Southern Island

Waitaki

Lake Wakatipu

Lake Te Anau

Clutha

●Dunedin

Foveaux Strait

Stewart Island

To Easter Island

0 miles 100

0 km 100

▲ Abel Tasman's ship was the first European vessel to reach New Zealand.

▼ A Maori in clothes made from kiwi feathers, like those worn before the Europeans arrived

How New Zealand Got its Name

In 1642 two Dutch ships sailed from the Dutch East Indies (now part of Indonesia) under the command of Abel Tasman. He was in search of a "Great South Land" sailors had talked about for centuries. After several months at sea, the vessels anchored in Golden Bay, in the northern part of the South Island. Local Maori came out in canoes to make the challenge: "Friend or foe?" Misunderstanding the question, the Dutch sailors replied by blowing trumpets, which the Maori interpreted as the response of an enemy. When a boat was lowered, the Maori attacked and four crewmen were killed. Tasman sailed away and no European was seen in New Zealand for another 127 years.

In 1769, the British explorer James Cook arrived at what he described in his journal as "the eastern side of the land discovered by Tasman." Perhaps Cook wanted to name the territory himself, but the Dutch sailors had already given the land a name—Nieuw Zeeland, after a region of the Netherlands.

On the Map

Cook saw smoke on shore as he sailed into a bay on the eastern coast of the North Island. He later named the area Poverty Bay, because he could not find any food to collect there. Cook literally put New Zealand on the map by spending six months sailing around the islands, making an incredibly accurate chart of their coastlines, which was used for the next 150 years. He did make mistakes, however. He thought Stewart Island was a peninsula and that Banks Peninsula, named for the botanist on Cook's ship, was an island.

▼ Actors reenact the moment when British sailors rowed to shore in 1770 at Ship Cove. James Cook named the cove in Marlborough Sounds on the South Island and used it as his base in the country.

Early Conflicts

Cook's maps were used first by European whaling ships, which came to the area to catch sperm whales. In 1814, Christian missionaries founded the first non-Maori settlements.

The Europeans brought the latest modern weapons with them, and the Maori were quick to realize their power. Between 1818 and 1836, the tribes fought between themselves in the terrible Musket Wars. These gradually ended as the missionaries successfully converted the Maori into peaceful Christians.

▲ Gold mines on the South Island attracted many European settlers despite the wars of the 1860s.

▼ British soldiers guard the remains of a Maori fort after the battle of Gate Pa in 1864.

In 1840, the Maori signed the Treaty of Waitangi, which made New Zealand a British colony. However, the fighting was far from over. In 1845, Hone Heke, a young Maori chief from Northland, cut down the British flag flying at Russell, near Waitangi. His protest against the European settlers taking away all the best land in the area led to the Flagstaff War, the first of five conflicts now known as the New Zealand, or Maori, Wars. The fighting was most intense in the 1860s, and peace was finally achieved

WHAT'S IN WAITANGI?

The Treaty of Waitangi, an 1840 agreement between the Maori people and the British, was written in English. But the version signed by most of the Maori leaders was poorly translated. By signing, the chiefs handed over New Zealand to Victoria, the queen of England. In return the British guaranteed the "full, exclusive and undisturbed possession of their lands and estates, forests, fisheries and other properties which they may collectively or individually possess." The treaty also made the Maori British subjects, so they would have the same rights as the British settlers arriving to make New Zealand their home.

However, the Maori version of the treaty used the word that meant "governorship" instead of "sovereignty," so the Maori leaders did not understand that they were giving away their country for good. In any event, the treaty was never properly followed. European settlers hungry for land took what they wanted from the Maori. The Maori were sometimes forced to sell land, or simply had it seized.

Even today, the complications of the two versions still cause problems between the New Zealand communities. The government has formed a tribunal (a type of law court) to help interpret the legal meaning of the treaty, to compensate people for injustices in the past, and to negotiate the return of Maori land. In 1993 the government began to give money to the Maori, and later they also gave land.

In February of each year, New Zealand celebrates Waitangi Day, to remember the signing of the treaty. In recent years Maori unhappy with the settlements of the 1990s have attempted to disrupt the celebrations.

▼ **Maori men practice a traditional dance with canoe paddles before the Waitangi Day celebrations.**

A REBEL'S RELIGION

One of the most famous Maori resistance leaders, Te Kooti Rikirangi, led a band of rebel fighters with great success during the New Zealand Wars until he was captured in 1866 and exiled to the distant Chatham Islands. There he experienced visions, which led to the establishment of a new religion, *Ringatu*, which still has several thousand believers today. It is a Maori version of Christianity, drawing heavily on the Old Testament. Ringatu is Maori for "the uplifted hand," and Te Kooti used to dunk his own hand in phosphorus so it would glow as he preached in dark Maori meeting houses. In 1868 Te Kooti dramatically escaped on a stolen schooner. He continued to take on the government troops, fighting in an area of the mainland where the tribes had elected a Maori king. The fighting finally ended in 1872, and Te Kooti was pardoned several years later. However, his influence as prophet and healer continued until his death in 1893.

▲ Te Kooti (pronounced korti) Rikirangi used his religion to gather followers to fight the British.

in the 1870s. However, several Maori groups had their lands taken away after the wars, and some are still demanding to have them back.

Gold Fever

While fighting raged in the North Island, gold fever hit the South. The 1860s saw several big gold rushes to Otago, Marlborough, and the rugged west coast region. New Zealand's tiny population doubled as fortune-seekers flooded in from Britain, Australia, China, and other parts of Asia. The gold production in 1866 reached 24 tons (22 tonnes), and for nearly ten years gold was the country's biggest export. Even today, New Zealand still has a large gold mining industry, producing about 13 tons (12 tonnes) a year.

Creating Society

Despite its violent beginnings, New Zealand has a long history of being a fair country. Free education began in 1877, and soon after all adult males, both European and Maori, were given voting rights. In 1893, New Zealand was the first nation in the world to give women the vote, too.

Toward the end of the 1800s other social reforms took place, which laid the foundation for the good quality of life enjoyed by New Zealanders. (By the 1940s its people were wealthier than those of most other countries.) The hours people were made to work

▼ Families bound for a new life in New Zealand pose on board a passenger ship at Cork, Ireland, in 1895.

AN OFF-SHORE FARM

▲ Frozen sheep are unloaded from a New Zealand refrigerated ship at London's docks in 1947.

New Zealand's farms have always been very productive, but in the 1800s food rotted during the long journey to foreign markets. The solution was to freeze the food. In 1882 the first shipment of frozen meat arrived in Britain from New Zealand, after a dangerous voyage aboard the iron-hulled steamer *Dunedin*. Five thousand sheep carcasses were frozen on board using newly invented machinery. The meat took 98 days to arrive but was still in good condition. It was sold to British consumers at a price far higher than it could have reached in New Zealand.

Voyages like this soon became an important source of affordable food for Britain's growing population. It was also a turning point for the New Zealand economy, as farmers began to breed sheep for meat as well as wool. The *Dunedin* made nine more voyages but sunk in 1890, probably after running into an iceberg near Cape Horn in South America.

were reduced. The world's first labor arbitration system was established. This forced workers and employers to discuss labor problems without calling strikes.

National Identity

World War I (1914–1918) caused New Zealanders to feel they belonged to a country in its own right, not a colony of Britain. The country suffered huge losses while fighting for Britain. There were 60,000 casualties on France's Western Front alone, more than a quarter of all the men of fighting age living in the country at the time. Nevertheless, many New Zealanders still called Britain "home." New Zealand had been a self-governing "dominion" since 1907. In the 1930s, it was given the option to become fully independent from Britain, but at that time few people were interested.

New Zealanders again fought bravely in World War II (1939–1945). The heaviest fighting of all was during the Battle of Crete in 1941 when New Zealanders, both European and Maori, defended the Greek island from German paratroopers. Although the New Zealanders lost the battle, it consolidated the still-young nation's pride in being "Kiwis." In 1947, the New Zealand government finally decided to make the country fully independent in its own right.

▲ A New Zealand soldier and Maori warrior both pay their respects at a World War I memorial in France.

A FULL WELFARE STATE

I n the 1930s the leader of the Labour Party, Michael Joseph Savage (right), made New Zealand the world's first full welfare state. Under this system, taxes were used to pay for a national health service that provided free medicines and medical care to everyone. Poor families were given extra money by the government. Soon other governments all over the world were copying New Zealand's policy.

Living
on the
Edge

NEW ZEALAND USED TO FEEL A LONG WAY from everywhere else—it appears in the far bottom corner of most world maps. Foreigners visiting the country sometimes compared it to Britain, only stuck in the 1950s. In the 1970s and '80s, many young people chose to leave for a few years for "OE" (overseas experience).

Nevertheless, even then New Zealand had its own cultural identity, formed in the last 150 years as Maori traditions fused with the ways of the *Pakeha*, the Maori name for European New Zealanders. Modern air travel now makes it possible to fly to New Zealand from anywhere in less than 24 hours. Today the country is thoroughly modern with new influences from many lands mixing with the islands' traditional culture.

◀ People dressed in outlandish costumes parade through the streets of Auckland during the annual Farmers' Santa Parade, the largest city event in New Zealand.

URBAN AND RURAL POPULATION

An old joke about the country having far more sheep than people may still be true, but there are now four million New Zealanders. The typical Kiwi is no longer a farmer striding out to check animals grazing on his land, because a staggering 86 percent of the population lives in cities. A third of them live in the Auckland area. This city is the country's largest and has more people living in it than the whole of the South Island. Auckland is home to many of the country's latest arrivals from East Asia, Africa, and the Pacific islands (other than the Maori). Maori numbers dropped by two-thirds through diseases and wars when Europeans arrived, but their population is currently increasing, forming 15 percent of New Zealanders.

▲ A view of Auckland from the city's Sky Tower. At 1,076 feet (328 m), this building is the tallest structure in the Southern Hemisphere.

Common New Zealand Phrases

Here are a few words and phrases you might use in New Zealand. Maori words are pronounced as they are spelled:

Bach	A holiday home, pronounced "batch"
Bludger	Someone who doesn't pay his or her way
Hongi	Maori greeting with pressed noses
Cocky	A farmer
Pakeha	A non Maori
Pom	Someone from Britain
Section	Land surrounding a house
She'll be right	Everything will work out
Shoot through	Leave
Wop-wops	Remote areas

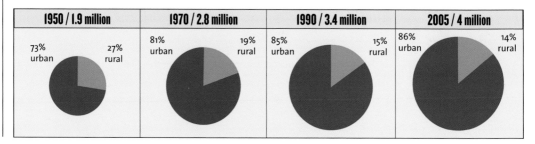

1950 / 1.9 million	1970 / 2.8 million	1990 / 3.4 million	2005 / 4 million
73% urban — 27% rural	81% urban — 19% rural	85% urban — 15% rural	86% urban — 14% rural

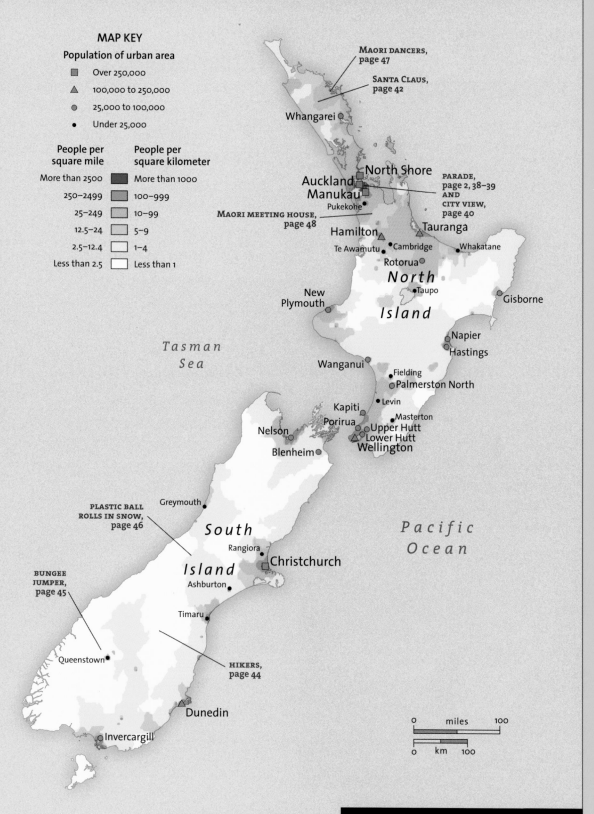

MAP KEY

Population of urban area

- ■ Over 250,000
- ▲ 100,000 to 250,000
- ● 25,000 to 100,000
- • Under 25,000

People per square mile	People per square kilometer
More than 2500	More than 1000
250–2499	100–999
25–249	10–99
12.5–24	5–9
2.5–12.4	1–4
Less than 2.5	Less than 1

MAORI DANCERS, page 47

SANTA CLAUS, page 42

Whangarei

North Shore

Auckland
Manukau

PARADE, page 2, 38–39 AND CITY VIEW, page 40

Pukekohe

MAORI MEETING HOUSE, page 48

Hamilton

Tauranga

Te Awamutu   Cambridge   Whakatane

Rotorua

North

Taupo

Island

New Plymouth

Gisborne

Napier
Hastings

Tasman Sea

Wanganui

Fielding
Palmerston North

Kapiti   Levin

Porirua   Masterton

Nelson   Upper Hutt
Lower Hutt
Wellington

Blenheim

Greymouth

PLASTIC BALL ROLLS IN SNOW, page 46

South

Rangiora

Island   Christchurch

BUNGEE JUMPER, page 45

Ashburton

Pacific Ocean

Timaru

Queenstown

HIKERS, page 44

Dunedin

Invercargill

0   miles   100

0   km   100

Population Map

NATIONAL HOLIDAYS

The list of holidays in New Zealand is similar to that of a European or North American country. It includes the main Christian festivals and a day off for New Year's. However, celebrating these events is somewhat different in New Zealand because its seasons are at the opposite times of year from the Northern Hemisphere. Christmas is at the height of summer, but that does not stop people from dressing in Santa Claus costumes (below) as part of the fun! New Zealand also honors its soldiers (along with Australia) on Anzac Day, while the treaty that brought New Zealand into existence is celebrated on Waitangi Day.

JANUARY 1	New Year's Day
FEBRUARY 6	Waitangi Day
MARCH/APRIL	Easter
APRIL 25	Anzac Day
FIRST MONDAY IN JUNE	Queen's Birthday
FOURTH MONDAY IN OCTOBER	Labour Day
DECEMBER 25	Christmas Day
DECEMBER 26	Boxing Day

Regional Differences

New Zealand is a small country, and the lifestyle in one region is very much like that of another. However, the North Island is most heavily populated, with three-quarters of all New Zealanders. As a result it is considered to be more enterprising and fast-paced. The South Island has a slower pace of life than the north and a more rural lifestyle.

The west coast of the South Island attracts people looking for life in a remote and rugged region. They are proud of their pioneering spirit, like those who came to the region in the gold-rush days of the 1860s. The island's east coast is home to communities of farmers who live on sheep ranches, or stations.

The New Zealand countryside is very thinly peopled—the west coast of the South Islands has fewer than 6 people per square mile (2 per square km). The number of

I DIE, I LIVE!

Haka is the Maori word for "dance," but nowadays it usually refers to ferocious war chants performed by New Zealand's national teams to intimidate the opposition before their matches—usually with great success! The most famous hakas are made by the national rugby team, the All Blacks. The use of hands, feet, legs, tongue, and eyes are as important as the actual words. The usual haka begins with the words Ka mate! Ka mate! (I die! I die!), Ka ora! Ka ora! (I live! I live!), but the rugby team also uses a newer version, called *Kapa o Pango* (Team in Black).

▲ **The All Blacks perform their terrifying haka before a match.**

country villages is decreasing, and most towns have populations of more than 10,000. The largest cities are Auckland and Wellington (the capital) in the North Island, and Christchurch and Dunedin in the South Island. Today nearly all Maori live in the cities of the North Island.

Rugby Fever

The favorite sport of New Zealand is rugby. Many men and women play it, but nearly everyone enjoys watching the national team, the All Blacks, play around the world. This team plays in black uniforms and its success forms an important part of how New Zealanders see themselves. They are rightly proud

that a nation of just four million can produce a team that can beat those of much larger countries, such as England and France. If the team performs badly, Aotearoa changes into "The Land of the Long Black Cloud," rather than the white, while

people recover from the disappointment.

Rugby became the main winter sport more than 100 years ago. New Zealand's boys learn to play this rough and tough game at an early age. Many of the top All Blacks players are Maori, who channel their warrior traditions into this fast and often furious sport.

Other sports popular in New Zealand are cricket, sailing, and hiking (known in New Zealand as "tramping"), often along designated tracks in national parks. In the mountains, people go whitewater canoeing, as well as skiing and mountaineering in winter. The first man to scale Mount Everest was New Zealander Sir Edmund Hillary, who learned to climb in the Southern Alps.

Outdoor Living

With so much amazing scenery in the country

and plenty of space at their disposal, New Zealanders spend a lot of time outdoors. Most houses have a large garden or plot of land, known as a "section," surrounding them. Often a garden will have a covered area used for shelter from the rain. Whatever the weather, it is not uncommon to see a family grilling food outdoors on a gas or charcoal barbeque, or "barbie."

Eating, New Zealand Style

Until New Zealanders began to travel to other countries and sample different foods, most of their meals were traditional British dishes, such as roasted meat and boiled vegetables, meat pies, or fish fried in batter with "chips"—chunky french fries. This is what

TAKING THE PLUNGE

Maximum fun, minimum risk, is how New Zealanders advertise the daredevil adventure sport bungee jumping, which the Kiwis have made their own. It involves plunging earthward from high platforms with only a strong rubber cord strapped to the ankles or a body harness. The craze began when a Kiwi bungee jumped from the Eiffel Tower in Paris and came home to set up the world's first commercial operation at Queenstown in 1988. Jumpers descended from a 141-foot (43-m) bridge. Now there are several similar sites in the area, often above scenic canyons and rivers. A rigorous safety code makes it a very safe experience. People who have made the ten-second drop, which is often videotaped as a souvenir, say they get a feeling of exhilaration that lasts for days.

▲ A jumper makes a giant leap above Lake Wakatipu, near Queenstown.

▲ A person rolls down a slope in a "zorb"—a padded plastic ball. Zorbing is another adventure sport invented in New Zealand.

people's ancestors had eaten in "the Old Country."

In the last 30 years New Zealand cooking has changed a great deal. The country's high-quality meats and vegetables are still used, but people now also cook dishes influenced by the spicy flavors of the Pacific Rim and Southeast Asia. The oceans around New Zealand are rich with seafood such as mussels, which are now also a common food.

The Maori never lost the art of their traditional use of the *hangi* (earth oven), where food is cooked in a hole in the ground over heated stones. Potatoes, *kumara* (a New Zealand sweet potato), pumpkin, corn, carrots, poultry, fish, and meats are steamed until tender, the food taking on some of the flavor of the earth. Hangi are used to prepare the food for most formal Maori occasions, such as weddings and birthdays.

FROM MIDDLE EARTH

▲ Characters from *Lord of the Rings* arrive at the movie's premier in Wellington.

New Zealand has its share of Hollywood stars. Oscar winners Russell Crowe and Anna Paquin were born in the country. Maori actor Temuera Morrison was cast as bounty hunter Jango Fett in *Star Wars: Attack of the Clones.* His warrior character was cloned to produce the Empire's force of stormtroopers. Oscar-winning director Peter Jackson chose New Zealand, his home country, to be the fantasy land of Middle Earth in his *Lord of the Rings* films. Scenes were filmed at over 150 locations, including in national parks, where the Department of Conservation ensured sets were dismantled immediately afterward and the land was restored to its original state. Hobbiton was set in the rolling hills near Matamata, in the North Island's Waikato, while Mount Ruapehu doubled for Mount Doom.

Maoritanga: Maori Culture

The word *Maori* is not the name of a nation or people. It just means "normal" in the language of the first New Zealanders. Despite the many wars and other disruptions caused by the colonization of their lands, the Maori have kept their arts, crafts, songs, and dances alive, and they still form a strong source of pride. The Maori have no writing; their history was recorded in songs and chants. The actions for each song also form

part of its meaning. The *poi* dance is unique to New Zealand Maori, where dancers swing poi (balls made from raupo, a type of bulrush, tied onto the end of a cord).

▲ Maori women dance holding poi, two fluffy, white balls swung on a cord.

Carving Wood and Stone...

The Maori are skilled carvers and still make beautiful war canoes (*waka*) from the wood of native trees. The center of a Maori community is its meeting house, a large wooden building with a single room. These are also decorated with fine wooden carvings.

Greenstone (a type of jade) is soft enough to be carved, even with traditional bone and wood tools, and it is still worked today. The Maori name for this mineral is *pounamu*. It is found mainly on the South Island's west coast and was once used to make war clubs (*mere*).

Today, greenstone studios and workshops turn out small sculptures in a Maori style. The most frequently seen carving is the *tiki*, which means "the hanging human form." These tiny Maori figures are worn on a string or chain around the neck, and are considered to have great power.

▲ A tiki pendant, carved from greenstone, is one of the most famous Maori symbols.

▼ A Maori elder sits in an ornate meeting house wearing a ceremonial cloak and holding a fighting stick, or *taiaha*.

...*and Skin!*

High-ranking Maori traditionally showed their rank with *moko* patterns on their faces, arms, and torso. These look like dark tattoos but they are made by carving grooves into the skin with a bone chisel rather than dyeing under the skin through thin cuts. Moko appear on the bodies of some Maori today, and their style of patterns has become popular in the body art produced around the world.

THE MAORI NIGHTINGALE

One of the world's most famous New Zealanders in Kiri Te Kanawa, a world-class opera singer. Kiri was born in Gisborne, North Island, in 1944. She has both Maori and European ancestry. Kiri's magnificent voice was discovered in a singing competition in 1965. The first prize was a chance to study music in England. Soon Kiri was performing at London's opera houses. Her career has since taken her all over the world, and she is often booked to perform five years in advance. Despite her international successes, Kiri is very committed to her New Zealand roots and has set up a foundation to help young singers and musicians in the country.

▲ Dame Kiri Te Kanawa performs in Lebanon.

Sacred Places

Respect for Maori culture is growing steadily in New Zealand, and most Pakeha now understand how to treat sacred Maori sites. One of their most sacred places is at the far tip of the North Island, where Cape

▼ A meeting house carving tells how the world was created by Tane, the god of the forest and son of the sky and Earth.

Reinga stretches out into the Pacific Ocean and Tasman Sea. The Maori believe that a dead person's soul comes here and slides down the roots of an old *pohutukawa* tree—which is still in place— and then rejoins the spirits of the ancestors in the ancient homeland of Hawaiki.

Going It Alone

UNTIL THE 1990s THE GOVERNMENT of New Zealand played the main role in running the nation's economy. This was because of the country's strong tradition of ensuring that everyone has a good standard of living, including the unemployed and the sick. However, New Zealand ran into trouble in the 1970s, when its main trading partner, Britain, began to buy its food from Europe. With this strong trading link broken, New Zealand's economy collapsed, and by the end of the 1980s, more than a third of its people were supported by money from the government. But a series of bold economic changes in the 1990s proved very successful, and today the country is a fantastic place to live, with a relaxed way of life and high standard of living.

◀ Sheep cover a hillside on a station, or ranch, near Christchurch. At one time, New Zealand lamb and wool was sent just to Britain, but today it is sold across the world.

A LINK TO THE OLD COUNTRY

New Zealand has been independent for 60 years, but its head of state is still the British monarch (king or queen). Queen Elizabeth II seldom visits the country, but her representative is the Governor General. This position is currently held by Anand Satyanand. He was appointed by the queen on the advice of New Zealand's prime minister. He has largely ceremonial duties but also has powers to take over the country during a constitutional crisis.

▶ Prince William, second in line to the British throne, is escorted by Silvia Cartwright, the previous Governor General, during a visit to New Zealand in 2005. One day William may be the head of state of New Zealand.

Trade Partners

It is not surprising that New Zealand's largest trading partner is its neighbor Australia. A fifth of all New Zealand goods exported (sold abroad) are sent to Australia. A similar amount of goods comes back the other way.

New Zealand's biggest exports are food, mainly beef and lamb, dairy products, and fruits. The country is also one of the few places in the South Pacific that has fast-growing forests suitable for making wood and paper, which are also big export products. New Zealand imports highly engineered machines, such as cars and computers, and much of its fuel.

Country	Percent New Zealand exports
Australia	20.7%
United States	14.9%
Japan	11.5%
China	5.0%
All others combined	47.9%

Country	Percent New Zealand imports
Australia	22.6%
United States	12.6%
Japan	12.1%
China	8.4%
All others combined	44.3%

NORTHLAND

⊙Whangarei

*Tasman
Sea*

AUCKLAND

Auckland⊙

Hamilton⊙

WAIKATO

Whakatane⊙

BAY OF
PLENTY

*North
Island*

GISBORNE

Gisborne⊙

Stratford⊙

TARANAKI

HAWKE'S
BAY

MANAWATU-
WANGANUI

Napier⊙

WOOL WAREHOUSE,
page 56

PRINCE WILLIAM,
page 52

Palmerston North⊙

NELSON

TASMAN

Nelson⊙

WELLINGTON

Richmond⊙

⊛ Wellington

Blenheim⊙

MARLBOROUGH

WEST
COAST

WHALE WATCHERS,
page 55

Greymouth⊙

*South
Island*

SHEEP FARM,
page 3, 50–51

CANTERBURY

Christchurch⊙

*Pacific
Ocean*

OTAGO

SOUTHLAND

Dunedin⊙

Invercargill⊙

Political Map

Tops for Tourism

Where once the New Zealand economy was powered by cattle and sheep farmers, today it relies on backpackers, thrill seekers, and whales. Tourism is now the country's single largest industry, employing more than 100,000 New Zealanders. Tourism is helped by a strong image of New Zealand abroad as a beautiful and friendly place. The cost of getting to this distant land is also cheaper than ever. Every year more than two million foreigners visit. Most come from Australia, the United Kingdom, and Japan.

HOW THE GOVERNMENT WORKS

New Zealand has a parliamentary form of government based on the system used in Britain. Like Britain it has no written constitution. Laws are passed by a parliament containing just one group of lawmakers. The House of Representatives is based in Wellington, and its members are elected for three-year terms. Everyone over the age of 18 has a vote. There are 122 seats in the House, seven of which are reserved for the Maori, who are elected by separate Maori voters. However, Maori candidates have also been elected to non-reserved seats. There are two main parties, National and Labour, with several minor ones. The party that has the most elected representatives forms the government. The leader of this party becomes Prime Minister. In 2004, the Supreme Court became the highest court in New Zealand, taking over from the British "Law Lords" based in London. Supreme Court judges are appointed by the Prime Minister.

GOVERNOR GENERAL		
EXECUTIVE	LEGISLATIVE	JUDICIARY
PRIME MINISTER	PARLIAMENT	SUPREME COURT
CABINET OF MINISTERS	HOUSE OF REPRESENTATIVES (122)	HIGH COURT

A Furry Friend

New Zealand is famous for producing a sweet, green fruit with a furry brown skin known as the Chinese gooseberry. The fruit is now so closely linked with the country that its original name has been replaced with a more suitable one—kiwifruit.

Seeds for the kiwifruit vine were first brought to New Zealand in the early 20th century by a teacher who had been visiting schools in China. At first it was grown as a garden plant, and few people ate its fruit. In the 1980s the fruit's potential was realized. The fruits are exported in coolers aboard ships, where they slowly ripen in time for arrival at their destinations. Most orchards are in the North Island, especially around the Bay of Plenty. Other fruits are grown in Hawke's Bay, dubbed the country's "fruit bowl."

▲ Tourists enjoy the sight of the enormous tail of a sperm whale off the east coast of the South Island near Kaikoura.

▼ Kiwifruits are an excellent source of vitamin C, even after the long journey by sea from New Zealand.

In the Neighborhood

New Zealand's economy has been helped by its strong trading links with Australia: the pair have a trade agreement that reduces the cost of selling things to each other. However, relations between the two Down-Under neighbors have always been rather edgy. The two peoples can be very critical of each other. Occasionally there are sharp disputes involving sporting incidents or business links. Some Australians seem to regard New Zealand as being a more backward and provincial, less-sophisticated society than their own, while New Zealanders think "Oz" is just bigger and brasher and its people too opinionated. However, outsiders find it hard to tell the difference between the two peoples.

The Australian Constitution makes it possible for New Zealand to become its seventh state, but there is no prospect of any political union between the two countries. However, Kiwis that opt to live abroad more often choose to make nearby Australia their new home,

▲ Bales of wool are inspected for quality before being loaded onto a ship at Napier, a major port in the North Island.

THE GREAT DESSERT DEBATE

Kiwifruit is the must-use garnish for a unique delicious New Zealand pudding, the Pavlova—a crunchy-yet-soft meringue base topped with thick whipped cream and sliced fruits (right). However, Australians also claim the "Pav" as their creation. The debate rages on, just one of many causes of dispute between the two neighbors.

INDUSTRY MAP

I t does not make sense to manufacture things in New Zealand. It would be too expensive to import raw materials and just as pricey to export products to be sold abroad. As a result New Zealand does not have many factories. The biggest heavy industry is mining, which is located mainly in the South Island. The mines produce gold, coal, and iron ore.

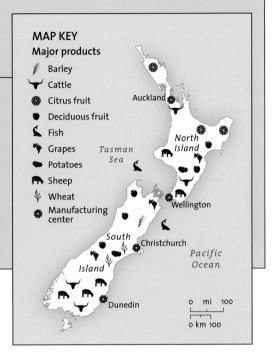

MAP KEY
Major products

- Barley
- Cattle
- Citrus fruit
- Deciduous fruit
- Fish
- Grapes
- Potatoes
- Sheep
- Wheat
- Manufacturing center

Auckland

North Island

Tasman Sea

Wellington

South Island

Christchurch

Pacific Ocean

Dunedin

0 mi 100
0 km 100

rather than the United Kingdom, where many of them also have the right to live.

Changing Times

In the 1990s many of the New Zealand government's services were turned into businesses. This move was an attempt to make the country run more efficiently. After a period of hardship for its people, the country now has a booming economy. Farmers are selling food to new markets in Asia. High-tech companies can now compete with those in other countries. Thanks to high-speed communications through the Internet it does not matter that their colleagues are on the other side of the world. As a result the country has become a very attractive place to live and work.

▼ The rivalry between New Zealand and Australia is often played out on the sports field. When it comes to cricket, Australia (green and yellow) normally wins.

Add a Little Extra to Your Country Report!

I f you are assigned to write a report about New Zealand, you'll want to include basic information about the country, of course. The Fast Facts chart on page 8 will give you a good start. The rest of the book will give you the details you need to create a full and up-to-date paper or PowerPoint presentation. But what can you do to make your report more fun than anyone else's? If you use your imagination and dig a bit deeper into some of the topics introduced in this book, you're sure to come up with information that will make your report unique!

>Flag

Perhaps you could explain the history of New Zealand's flag, and the meanings of its colors and symbols. Go to **www.crwflags.com/fotw/flags** for more information.

>National Anthem

How about downloading New Zealand's national anthem, and playing it for your class? At **www.nationalanthems.info** you'll find what you need, including the words to the anthem, plus sheet music fo it. Simply pick "N" and then "New Zealand" from the list on the left-hand side of the screen, and you're on your way.

>Time Difference

If you want to understand the time difference between New Zealand and where you are, this Web site can help: **www.worldtimeserver.com**. Just pick "New Zealand" from the list on the left. If you called someone in New Zealand right now, would you wake them up from their sleep?

>Currency

Another Web site will convert your money into dollars, the currency used in New Zealand. You'll want to know how much money to bring if you're ever lucky enough to travel to New Zealand: **www.xe.com/ucc**.

>Weather

Why not check the current weather in New Zealand? It's easy—go to **www.weather.com** to find out if it's sunny or cloudy, warm or cold in New Zealand right now! Pick "World" from the headings at the top of the page. Then search for the New Zealand. Click on any city. Be sure to click on the tabs below the weather report for Sunrise/Sunset information, Weather Watch, and Business Travel Outlook, too. Scroll down the page for the 36-Hour Forecast and a satellite weather map. Compare your weather to the weather in the New Zealand city you chose. Is this a good season, weather-wise, for a person to travel to New Zealand?

>Miscellaneous

Still want more information? Simply go to National Geographic's World Atlas for Young Explorers at **http://www.nationalgeographic.com/ kids-world.atlas**. It will help you find maps, photos, music, games, and other features that you can use to jazz up your report.

Glossary

Cabinet a group of politicians who run a country. Each member of the cabinet is called a minister and is in charge of a particular part of the government.

Ceremonial a duty or ritual that is performed as a symbol of a belief or a power but has no other useful purpose.

Climate the average weather of a certain place at different times of year.

Colony a region that is ruled by a nation located somewhere else in the world. Settlers from that distant country take the land from the region's original inhabitants.

Conservation protecting plants and animals that are becoming rare.

Culture a collection of beliefs, traditions, and styles that belongs to people living in a certain part of the world.

Democracy a country that is ruled by a government chosen by all its people through elections.

Dominion a country that belongs to the British Commonwealth and whose head of state is the British monarch.

Economy the system by which a country creates wealth through making and trading in products.

Endangered an animal or plant that is at risk of dying out.

Exported transported and sold outside the country of origin.

Geothermal a source of heat from deep underground. Geothermal power plants tap this energy to make electricity.

Glacier a body of ice formed over thousands of years, mainly by layers of snow, that slowly flows on land.

Gold rush when many miners and adventurers head for the same location to try to find large amounts of gold.

Governor General someone who governs a territory on behalf of a more senior ruler. New Zealand's Governor General represents the British monarch in affairs of state.

Hemisphere one half of a sphere, or globe. The Earth is generally divided into the Northern and Southern Hemisphere. New Zealand is in the Southern Hemisphere.

Imported brought into the country from abroad.

Peninsula a narrow piece of land that is surrounded by water on three sides. The word means "almost island" in Latin.

Rural an area that has large areas of country-side and farmland. Rural areas have fewer people than urban places.

Species a type of organism; animals or plants in the same species look similar and can only breed successfully among themselves.

Treaty a written agreement between two or more countries. Treaties are made to end wars or organize trade.

Urban an area that has many buildings and is crowded with people.

Union an agreement between regions or countries to join together as a single state.

Welfare state a social-security system that provides money and housing for people who do not have jobs or are too ill to work.

Bibliography

Britton, Tamara. *New Zealand*. Edina, MN: Abdo Publishing, 2004.

Gillespie, Carol Ann. *New Zealand*. Philadelphia, PA: Chelsea House Publishers, 2002.

Yip, Dora. *Welcome to New Zealand*. Milwaukee, WI: Gareth Stevens Publishing, 2002.

http://newzealand.govt.nz/ aboutnz/at-a glance/ (facts and figures about the country from the official web site of New Zealand's government)

http://www.parliament.nz/ en-NZ/HstBldgs/ (historical information about New Zealand's parliament)

Further Information

NATIONAL GEOGRAPHIC Articles

Warne, Kennedy. "The Global Fish Crisis: Blue Haven." NATIONAL GEOGRAPHIC (April 2007): 70–89.

Web sites to explore

More fast facts about New Zealand, from the CIA (Central Intelligence Agency): https://www.cia.gov/library/ publications/the-world-fact-book/geos/nz.html

Hell's Gate, the most active geothermal area of Rotorua, is at the center of the North Island's volcanic region. Take a virtual tour or watch an explanatory video: http://www.hellsgate.co. nz/Hells_Gate/General_ Overview_IDL=2_IDT=627_ ID=3491_.html

See the New Zealand rugby union team—the All Blacks—perform the Haka war dance before a game. In this clip, they are playing Tonga, another team with Polynesian traditions, which responds to the Haka with their own war dance: http:// youtube.com/ watch?v=8eGCsEQ15L4& feature=related

Visit the Glowworm Cavern at the Waitomo caves through your computer. Look at a 360° panorama of the cave with the glowworms clearly in view. The same Web site also has other panoramas from New Zealand including Fox Glacier in the Southern Alps and a bungee jump in progress. You can even watch panoramic videos of a glider flight over Queenstown or a boat trip through Fiordland's Milford Sound: http://www.worldinmotionvr. com/samples/cubicvr/full/glow worm_full.html

See, hear

There are many ways to get a taste of life in New Zealand, such as movies and music. You might be able to locate these:

New Zealand Herald
Find out what is important in New Zealand today by checking out the Web site of one of the country's biggest newspapers: http://www. nzherald.co.nz/

Storytime Treasure Chest
Radio New Zealand often broadcasts children's stories. You can listen to some of them at http://www.radionz.co.nz/ national/programmes/ storytime_treasure_chest

Whale Rider (2002)
A family film from New Zealand about Pai, a 12-year-old Maori girl who is the only child of the tribe's chief.

Index

Credits

Picture Credits

Front Cover – Spine: Sasha Davas/Shutterstock; Top: John Eastcott and Yva Momatiuk/NGIC; Low Far Left: Todd Gipstein/NGIC; Low Left: Frans Lanting/NGIC; Low Right: W.A Rogers /NGIC; Low Far Right: Brian J. Skerry/ NGIC.

Interior – Corbis: Adnan Abidi/Reuters: 57 lo; Macduff Everton: 48 lo; David Gray/Reuters: 52 up; Hulton Deutsch: 42 up; Frans Lanting: 14 lo; David Lawrence: 13 up; Charles & Josette Lenars: 48 up; Greg Probst: 2 lo far left, 6; Jose Fuste Raga: 5 up; Paul A. Souders: TP; Uli Wiesmeier/Zefa: 12 lo; Getty Images: AFP: 11 up, 46 lo, 49 up; Hulton Archive: 30 up, 32 lo, 34 up, 35 lo, 36 up, 37 lo; ; Image Bank: 43 up, 56 lo; Hannah Johnston: 3 up, 33 lo, 38; Ross Land: 43 up; Colin Monteath: 10 left ; Pascal Le Segretain: 37 up; Roger Viollet: 28; Phil Walter: 42 lo; NGIC: James L. Amos: 3 far right, 50-51; Annie Griffiths Belt: 24 lo; Brian Brake/ Rapho Division: 49 lo; Mark Cosslet: 44 lo; John Eastcott and YVA Momatiuk: 20 up; Todd Gipstein: 40 left; Robert B. Goodman: 15; Herbert Kane: 2-3, 26-27; Anne Keiser: 44up; Frans Lanting: 2 left, 11 lo,12 up, 14 up,16-17, 18 lo, 21 up, 22, 23, 25, 30 lo; Bates Littlehales: 56 up; David Mclain: 45; Photo Archive: 31 lo, 47; Maria Stenzel: 55 up; NPL: Tim Edwards: 20 lo; Shutterstock: Sandra Caldwell: 55 lo; Steve Weaver 59 up.

For more information, please call 1-800-NGS-LINE (647-5463) or write to the following address:

NATIONAL GEOGRAPHIC SOCIETY
1145 17th Street N.W.
Washington, D.C. 20036-4688 U.S.A.

Visit us online at www.nationalgeographic.com/books

Library of Congress Cataloging-in-Publication Data available on request
ISBN: 978-1-4263-0301-2

Printed in the United States of America

Series design by Jim Hiscott.
The body text is set in Avenir; Knockout.
The display text is set in Matrix Script.

Front Cover—Top: Ngati Porou men ride horses at Anaura Bay, North Island; Low Far Left: Auckland from the Sky Tower; Low Left: Endangered kakapo parrot; Low Right: Maori carving; Low Far Right: Fiordland National Park

Page 1—Children at a swimming hole, Whangarel, North Island; Icon image on spine, Contents page, and throughout: Kiwi fruit

Produced through the worldwide resources of the National Geographic Society

John M. Fahey, Jr., *President and Chief Executive Officer*; Gilbert M. Grosvenor, *Chairman of the Board*; Tim T. Kelly, *President, Global Media Group*; John Q. Griffin, *President, Publishing*; Nina D. Hoffman, *Executive Vice President, President of Book Publishing Group*

National Geographic Staff for this Book

Nancy Laties Feresten, *Vice President, Editor-in-Chief of Children's Books*
Bea Jackson, *Director of Design and Illustration*
Jim Hiscott, *Art Director*
Virginia Koeth, *Project Editor*
Lori Epstein, *Illustrations Editor*
Stacy Gold, Nadia Hughes, *Illustrations Research Editors*
R. Gary Colbert, *Production Director*
Lewis R. Bassford, *Production Manager*
Nicole Elliott, *Manufacturing Manager*
Maps, *Mapping Specialists, Ltd.*

Brown Reference Group plc. Staff for this Book

Volume Editor: Tom Jackson
Designer: Dave Allen
Picture Manager: Clare Newman
Maps: Martin Darlison
Artwork: Darren Awuah
Index: Kay Ollerenshaw
Senior Managing Editor: Tim Cooke
Children's Publisher: Anne O'Daly
Editorial Director: Lindsey Lowe

About the Author

BARBARA JACKSON was born in New Zealand, the daughter of a dairy farmer, and was educated in Hamilton, Waikato province. She began a career in journalism in the country's largest city, Auckland, and now lives in London, England. Barbara has worked in the features department of three British newspapers and now specializes in travel writing for a number of magazines, frequently returning to New Zealand.

About the Consultants

VAUGHAN WOOD is a research fellow at the University of Canterbury, New Zealand. His main areas of research are agricultural history and environmental change in colonial New Zealand. He has also acted as a consultant on environmental issues for the Waitangi Tribunal in the indigenous land claims settlement process. He is working on a history of New Zealand's cocksfoot (orchardgrass) seed industry.

SIMON MILNE, a New Zealander, is director of the New Zealand Tourism Research Institute (www.tri.org.nz), Auckland University of Technology. He previously taught economic geography at McGill University, Canada. Professor Milne has spent more than 25 years researching economic development in the South Pacific region and elsewhere around the world. His research focuses on the links between tourism and sustainable economic development.

Time Line of New Zealand History

A.D.

ca 1000 Maori arrive from other parts of Polynesia.

1500

ca 1500 Maori build fortified sites, called *pa*, to defend themselves.

ca 1550 The Maori woodcarving tradition develops into its classic form.

1600

1642 Abel Tasman, a Dutch explorer, visits New Zealand but does not attempt to settle the islands after being attacked by Maori.

1700

1769 Captain James Cook, a British explorer, makes his first visit to New Zealand; on later trips, he maps the coastline.

1793 Maori visit New South Wales, in present-day Australia, and establish trade links.

1800

1814 Samuel Marsden establishes the first Christian mission in the Bay of Islands.

1815 Hongi Hika introduces muskets to Maori warfare and begins a 25-year series of conflicts known as the Musket Wars.

1830 Chiefs Te Rauparaha, Patuone, Nene, Moetara, and Tuwhare lead raids on the southern regions of New Zealand, near modern-day Port Nicholson.

1833 James Busby is appointed British Resident in New Zealand.

1835 Declaration of independence by the United Tribes of New Zealand is signed by 34 northern chiefs.

1837 The New Zealand Association is formed in London with the purpose of creating British settlements throughout New Zealand. It is renamed The New Zealand Company in 1839.

1840 Maori tribes sign the Treaty of Waitangi, which transfers the government of New Zealand to Great Britain but promises to protect Maori land.

1844 Hone Heke cuts down a British flagpole to protest British failure to respect the Treaty of Waitangi and begins the "War of the North."

1858 Te Wherwhero becomes the first Maori king, taking the name Potatau I.

1860 The New Zealand Wars begin as Governor Gore Browne orders British settlers to attack Maori settlements. The conflict becomes a 12-year civil war for the control of territory in the North Island.

1865 The capital moves from Auckland to Wellington.

1867 Four Maori seats are established in Parliament.

1870 The last British imperial forces leave New Zealand.

1888 The New Zealand parliament passes laws restricting Chinese immigration to the islands.